Bouquet de

PROVENCE

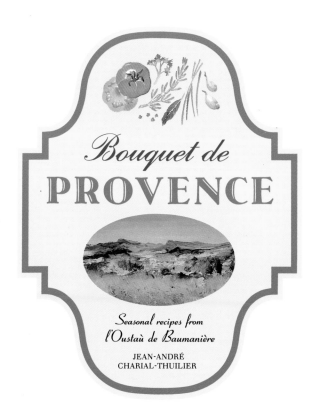

Bouquet de
PROVENCE

Seasonal recipes from
l'Oustaù de Baumanière

JEAN-ANDRÉ
CHARIAL-THUILIER

CLARKSON POTTER/PUBLISHERS

Provençal landscape illustrations copyright © 1990 by Raymond Thuilier
Recipe illustrations copyright © 1990
by Evie Safarewicz/John Hodgson Illustrators
Text copyright © 1990 by Jean-André Charial

Published by Clarkson N. Potter, Inc., 201 East 50th Street, New York,
New York, 10022.
Published in Great Britain by Pavilion Books Ltd. in 1990
CLARKSON POTTER, POTTER, and colophon are trademarks of Clarkson N.
Potter, Inc.
Manufactured in United Kingdom

Library of Congress Cataloging-in-Publication Data
Charial Thuilier, Jean-André, 1945–
Bouquet de Provence/Jean-André Charial-Thuilier

1. Cookery, France – Provençal style. 2. Cookery – France – Provence
3. Provence (France) – Social life and customs
I. Title
TX7 19.2.P75C47   1990
641.69449 – dc29   90–7436 CIP

ISBN 0–517–58045–4
10 9 8 7 6 5 4 3 2 1

First American Edition

*Cooks please note: American measurements appear
last in the ingredient lines of the recipes.*

CONTENTS

SPRING	9
SUMMER	35
AUTUMN	63
WINTER	91
ACKNOWLEDGEMENTS	117
INDEX	118

*E*arly morning on the Mediterranean: bright air resinous with Aleppo pine, water spraying over the gleaming tarmac of the Route Nationale and darkly reflecting the spring-summer green of the planes; swifts wheeling round the oleanders, waiters unpiling the wicker chairs and scrubbing the café tables; armfuls of carnations on the flower-stalls, pyramids of aubergines and lemons, *rascasses* on the fishmonger's slab goggling among the dark-wine urchins; smell of brioches from the bakeries . . .

Cyril Connolly, *The Unquiet Grave*

SPRING

Spring is the time of youth, when tender young vegetables flood the markets: broad beans, mange-touts, garden peas, artichokes, and asparagus from the village of Lauris on the banks of the Durance. Now, as the new season's lambs are reaching six or seven weeks old and the salmon are beginning their long journey back to the upper reaches of the Loire, is a time of blessings for cooks.

All the ingredients for lively, fresh-tasting spring-time dishes are now at hand – not forgetting that most essential one of all, the love and care which every good cook lavishes on their cooking. In one of Marcel Pagnol's *Marius* trilogy of plays set in Marseille, little Cesario protests at having to put on a pullover knitted for him by his grandmother because, he says, it is too scratchy. 'This pullover, you little nitwit,' César chides him, 'is not made with wool, but with love.'

And so it is with the art of cooking.

'*S*pring sprang suddenly onto the land. Green daffodils appeared above the grass. Wild rose bushes trembled beneath large blooms. The air was bitter and sharp as the fig tree's sap.'

Jean Giono, *Que ma joie demeure*

'*I*n April all the trees were in blossom. I was enchanted. Beneath a cherry tree I could see a ladder. A woman had climbed it, plunging head and hands in among the youngest leaves. Now and again, for no good reason, a great handful of petals would make their random departure. Floating from a cluster of flowers, they fell to the ground and scattered. The warm breeze awakened flowers, perfumes, insects, and went on to stir up the nests. There thousands of birds sang, throats open to the young wind, on that hill of gardens.'

Henri Bosco, *Le Jardin d'Hyacinthe*

SPRING

Menu

Artichoke Terrine with a Cream and Chive Sauce

Salmon with Olives

Leg of Lamb in Puff Pastry

Young Broad Beans with Mint

Hot Chocolate Creams

Asparagus Cream Soup with Oysters

Fresh Tuna à la Provençale

Roast Duck with Olives

Artichoke Hearts with Young Peas

Almond Tart with Pine Nuts

Artichoke Terrine with a Cream and Chive Sauce

TERRINE D'ARTICHAUTS À LA CRÈME DE CIBOULETTE

SERVES 8

4kg/9lb globe artichokes
1 tsp flour
chives
8 egg yolks
1 litre/1¾ pints/1 quart crème fraîche
salt and freshly ground white pepper
whipped cream, to serve

As the terrine needs to cool for 12 hours, it should be made the day before.

Preheat the oven to 200°C/400°F/gas mark 6.

Prepare a *bain-marie*: Select a rectangular oven-proof dish or roasting tin. Fill the dish or tin with water to a depth of 3cm/1¼ inches and place a sheet of newspaper folded in two in the bottom of the dish or tin to keep the water from boiling during cooking. Place the dish or tin in the oven and preheat it to its highest setting.

Prepare the artichokes by cutting away the leaves with scissors until only the hearts (*fonds*) are left.

Scrape away the hairy chokes. Cook the artichokes in boiling salted water containing the flour for about 30 minutes. Drain the artichokes and cut them in slices about 5mm/¼ inch thick. Arrange these in layers in the bottom of the terrine, adding a few chopped chives between the layers.

Beat the egg yolks into the *crème fraîche*, season to taste and pour this mixture over the artichokes. Put the terrine into the oven in the *bain-marie* and cook for about 30 minutes.

Leave to cool for 12 hours, then unmould and cut into slices. Serve with whipped cream, adding a few chopped chives before whipping.

Salmon with Olives

SAUMON AUX OLIVES

SERVES 4

4 slices salmon fillet, each 10cm/4 inches
wide, skin on
50ml/3½ tbsp sherry vinegar
50ml/3½ tbsp white wine
2 shallots
3 tbsp fish stock
salt and freshly ground black pepper
200g/7oz/1 cup black olives
1 tbsp crème fraîche
250g/9oz/2 sticks unsalted butter

TO COOK THE SALMON

Remove any bones from the salmon with tweezers.
Put the salmon slices in a non-stick frying pan, skin
side down, and cook over a low heat for about 10
minutes.

TO MAKE THE BEURRE BLANC

While the salmon is cooking, put the vinegar, wine, chopped shallots, fish stock and a pinch of salt in a small saucepan over a high heat. Boil to reduce until the liquid has almost completely evaporated.

Meanwhile, remove the stones from the black olives, then purée. Set aside.

Add the *crème fraîche* to the reduction and reduce again briefly. Lower the heat and little by little add the butter, kneaded with your fingers, whisking vigorously all the time until the sauce reaches a creamy consistency. Season to taste.

Remove from the heat. If the shallot has not melted entirely, sieve the sauce through a *chinois* (strainer).

Add the olive purée to the *beurre blanc* and mix together well.

TO SERVE

Remove the fish skin with a knife. Pour the sauce on to a dish and place the salmon in the middle.

Leg of Lamb in Puff Pastry

LE GIGOT D'AGNEAU EN CROÛTE

SERVES 2

1 very young leg of lamb, weighing
1kg/2¼lb or under if possible
2 lamb's kidneys
unsalted butter
100ml/4floz/½ cup Madeira
fresh or dried thyme
fresh or dried rosemary
salt and freshly ground black pepper
puff pastry
1 egg yolk

With a long, pointed knife, remove the bone from the leg of lamb. Cut the meat away from the bone until you reach the joint. Sever the joint and lift out the bone.

Preheat the oven to 270°C/500°F, or its highest setting.

Dice the kidneys finely and fry them in a little butter for about 3 minutes. Deglaze the frying pan with the Madeira, adding thyme and rosemary to taste.

Fill the cavity left by the bone with this mixture. Sew the leg of lamb together again and season it with salt and pepper. Put it in a roasting pan and rub a little butter over the lamb.

Put the lamb in the oven. Roast for about 15 minutes to seal the meat and draw out any water.

Roll out the puff pastry thinly to a size that is big enough to wrap up the lamb. Remove the lamb from the oven and wrap it in the puff pastry. Brush the top with the beaten egg yolk and return it to the oven for 10 minutes to finish cooking.

Young Broad Beans with Mint

FÈVES NOUVELLES À LA MENTHE FRAÎCHE

SERVES 4

2kg/4½lb young broad (fava) beans, shelled
200ml/7floz/1 cup double (heavy) cream
30ml/2 tbsp chopped fresh mint
salt and freshly ground black pepper

It is best to use young beans for this recipe as they are more tender and less floury than older beans. After you have shelled the beans you also need to skin them – a rather slow and fiddly job, but worth doing because the beans are so delicious.

Cook the beans in boiling salted water for 3–4 minutes, depending on their size, until just tender. Meanwhile, boil to reduce the cream in a sauté pan. Add the drained beans to the cream with the mint and seasoning to taste. Stir well, taking care not to crush the beans. Turn into a vegetable dish and serve.

Hot Chocolate Creams

FONDANT CHAUD AU CHOCOLAT

SERVES 4

75g/2½oz dark plain (semisweet)
chocolate
60g/2oz/4 tbsp unsalted butter
2 eggs
40g/1½oz/3 tbsp caster (superfine) sugar

FOR THE CRÈME ANGLAISE

1 vanilla bean
450ml/¾ pint/scant 2 cups milk
50ml/3½ tbsp crème fraîche
8 egg yolks
150g/5oz/½ cup caster (superfine) sugar

TO MAKE THE CRÈME ANGLAISE

If possible, make this the day before.

Crack open the vanilla pod lengthways. Put it in a heavy-based saucepan with the milk and *crème fraîche* and bring slowly to the boil. Remove from the heat immediately and leave to infuse for 30 minutes.

Meanwhile, in a bowl whisk together the egg yolks and sugar until the mixture begins to pale. Pour on the vanilla-flavoured milk gradually, stirring constantly, then return to the saucepan. Heat gently, but be careful not to let it boil: the *crème anglaise* is ready when it reaches 82°C/180°F exactly. If you do not have a thermometer, use a wooden spoon to test: the custard is ready when it is thick enough to coat the spoon and to hold the impression of your fingerprint when you touch it.

Strain through a *chinois* and refrigerate until needed.

TO MAKE THE CHOCOLATE CREAMS

Preheat the oven to 200°C/400°F/gas mark 6.

Melt the chocolate in a *bain-marie* (see page 14) or double boiler. Do the same with the butter until it is creamy. Beat the chocolate with the butter. Beat the eggs with the sugar just until the sugar has dissolved. Fold the chocolate mixture into the egg mixture.

Brush individual ramekins with melted butter and pour in the chocolate mixture. Place the ramekins on a baking sheet.

Bake for about 12 minutes or until just set: the centres should still be slightly liquid.

Leave to rest for 10 minutes before unmoulding on-to individual plates. Surround each cream with *crème anglaise* and serve.

Asparagus Cream Soup with Oysters

VELOUTÉ D'ASPERGES AUX HUITRES

SERVES 4

24 medium-sized spears asparagus
30g/1oz/2 tbsp unsalted butter
500ml/16floz/2 cups fish stock
50ml/16floz/2 cups crème fraîche
12 oysters
salt and freshly ground white pepper

Peel the asparagus stalks and wash in cold water. Cut off the tips and cook them in boiling salted water until tender. Drain and refresh by plunging into cold water. Drain well.

Dice the stalks and cook them gently in the butter in a large saucepan for about 3 minutes. Add the fish stock and simmer for about 20 minutes. Add the *crème fraîche* and simmer for 30 minutes or until the soup has a creamy consistency.

Open the oysters and remove them from their shells. Warm them in their own juices for a few moments. Do not overcook them or they will become tough.

Sieve the asparagus soup through a *chinois* (strainer). Adjust the seasoning, taking care not to add too much salt as the oysters are salty. Reheat the soup briefly.

Arrange 3 oysters and 6 asparagus tips in each soup plate and ladle the soup over. Serve hot.

Fresh Tuna à la Provençale

RÔTI DE THON FRAIS À LA PROVENÇALE

SERVES 4

8 small onions
200g/7oz button mushrooms
a handful of black olives
2 large plum tomatoes (about
300g/10oz total weight)
4 tbsp olive oil
a little butter
1kg/2¼lb fresh tuna, in one piece, skinned
salt and freshly ground black pepper
120ml/4floz/²⁄₃ cup white wine
fresh or dried thyme
fresh or dried tarragon

Peel the onions. Wash the mushrooms quickly, cut them in quarters and leave them to drain. Remove the stones from the olives. Skin, seed and chop the tomatoes.

In a cast-iron casserole, heat the olive oil with a small piece of butter over a high flame. Add the tuna and season with salt and pepper. Brown the fish on both sides, then lower the heat and cook, uncovered, for about 15 minutes. Add the white wine to deglaze the bottom of the casserole. Add the chopped tomatoes, a little thyme, a few tarragon leaves, the mushrooms, black olives and onions.

Cover the casserole and simmer over low heat for a good half hour. Use a heat diffuser, if necessary, to stop the mixture from burning.

Check if the fish is cooked and taste the sauce for proper seasoning. Remove the centre bone from the tuna, then place it on a warm dish. Pour the sauce over the fish. Serve with buttered noodles sprinkled with grated Gruyère or Parmesan.

Roast Duck with Olives

CANARD AUX OLIVES

SERVES 4

1 oven-ready duck, weighing 1.8kg/4lb
125g/4oz/²⁄₃ cup black olives (with
stones)
125g/4oz/²⁄₃ cup green olives (with
stones)
500ml/16floz/2 cups Madeira
salt and freshly ground black pepper
40g/1²⁄₃oz/2¹⁄₂ tbsp unsalted butter

FOR THE STOCK

2 carrots
1 onion
1 shallot
1 clove garlic
1 leek
1 stalk celery
20g/²⁄₃oz/4 tsp butter
500ml/16floz/2 cups red wine

Preheat the oven to 280°C/500°F or its highest
setting.

Peel the carrots, onion, shallot and garlic clove. Wash the leek and celery. Dice them all finely.

Remove the giblets from the duck as well as the neck, wing tips and feet. Chop into small pieces, keeping the liver to one side.

Put the butter in a saucepan and fry the vegetables and chopped giblet mixture (excluding the liver) gently for 5 minutes, until they start to brown. Add the red wine and 500ml/16fl oz water and keep at a rolling boil for about 30 minutes, skimming from time to time, until reduced by a quarter. Strain through a *chinois*.

TO ROAST THE DUCK

Roast the duck in the preheated oven for 40 minutes.

TO MAKE THE SAUCE

While the duck is cooking, remove the stones from all the olives and keep the stones. Blanch the green olives in boiling water for 5 minutes to lose their bitterness.

Put the Madeira and olive stones in a sauté pan and boil to reduce by half.

Add 250ml/8fl oz stock and reduce again, then add the finely chopped liver to thicken the sauce. Season to taste. Strain.

At the last minute, gradually add the butter in small pieces, whisking vigorously all the time over a very low heat. Add the olives.

Place the duck in a shallow serving dish and pour the sauce around it.

Artichoke Hearts with Young Peas

RAGOÛT DE FONDS D'ARTICHAUTS AUX PETIT POIS

100g/3¹/₂oz button mushrooms
few sprigs chervil
8 globe artichokes
1 lemon
vinegar
2 tbsp olive oil
salt and freshly ground black pepper
200g/7oz/1 cup tender young fresh green
peas, shelled

Wash the mushrooms and slice them finely. Chop the chervil.

To prepare the artichokes, first break off the stem close to the base. Starting from the bottom, remove the first few layers of hard leaves, then cut the artichoke across about halfway up, just above the heart. Using a small stainless steel knife, trim the artichoke all round, starting from the stem, to remove all the hard green parts and expose the paler heart (*fond*). Do the same to the top of the artichoke until the choke is revealed. Remove the choke with the

fingers or a spoon. Rub all the cut parts with lemon juice as you go along in order to prevent them from discolouring, then plunge the artichoke into water containing a dash of vinegar while you prepare the rest.

Drain the artichoke hearts and cut into quarters. Put them in a heavy-bottomed cast-iron saucepan with the olive oil. Season with salt and pepper, then cover and cook over a low heat for 15 minutes.

Add the peas, cover again and continue cooking for 10 minutes. Add the mushrooms and cook for another 5 minutes, still over a low heat.

Turn into a serving dish and sprinkle with the chopped chervil.

Almond Tart with Pine Nuts

TARTE AUX PIGNONS

SERVES 4–6

FOR THE PÂTE SABLÉE

150g/5oz/10 tbsp unsalted butter
250g/9oz/1¾ cups plain (all-purpose) flour
30g/1oz/⅓ cup ground almonds
90g/3oz/6 tbsp caster (superfine) sugar
1 egg

FOR THE ALMOND CREAM

100g/3½oz/7 tbsp unsalted butter
100g/3½oz/½ cup caster (superfine) sugar
100g/3½oz/1¼ cups ground almonds
2 eggs
2 tbsp rum
20g/⅔oz/3½ tbsp pine nuts

Take the butter out of the refrigerator in time to allow it to come to room temperature so that it is easier to work with.

Preheat the oven to 180°C/350°F/gas mark 4.

TO MAKE THE PÂTE SABLÉE

Beat the butter until soft. Rub together the butter, flour, ground almonds and 60g/2oz/¼ cup of the sugar, working quickly and lightly. This process is called *sablage* (sanding) in French.

Add the rest of the sugar and the egg and mix together lightly, just until the ingredients form a paste. If the *sablage* or mixing is too thorough, the pastry will not be of the right consistency and heavy.

Roll out the pastry with a rolling pin, preferably on a cool marble slab, and use to line a 20–23cm/8–9 inch tart tin.

TO MAKE THE ALMOND CREAM

Cream the butter in a bowl until it is light and smooth. Beat in the sugar, then the ground almonds. Beat the mixture well until the ingredients are evenly distributed.

Add one of the eggs and beat again for 3 or 4 minutes, until the mixture begins to increase in volume. Add the second egg and beat for another 3 or 4 minutes. Stir in the rum (or another spirit or liqueur if preferred, perhaps Grand Marnier or kirsch).

Spread the almond cream in the pastry case and scatter over the pine nuts, pushing them into the cream slightly so that they stay in place during cooking.

Bake in the preheated oven for 30–40 minutes, until risen and brown. Cool before serving.

'The southern country flushes to tender spring green only here and there. The cultivated hillsides keep their darker colours, though they may be most sweetly lit with the pink of almonds. March would be a glorious month in Provence if it were only for the almond blossom. Mixed with the soft grey of the olives it makes delicious pictures and it is to be found everywhere. And the wild rosemary is in flower – great bushes of it, lighting up the rocky hillsides with their delicate blue. They were all around me as I sat on this height, and there were brooms getting ready to flower, and wild lavender, and thyme. The air held an aromatic fragrance . . .'

Archibald Marshall, *A Spring Walk in Provence*

'*I* knew nothing of that serene season's invasion and conquest, that lasting treaty between warmth, colour and smell.'

Colette, *Bella-Vista*

Summer

Summer is the season of plenty in the kitchen garden: now fruit and vegetables are reaching their peak of ripeness and maturity, and the market stalls are brimming over with a magnificent harvest of green beans, aubergines, tomatoes, courgettes, salads of all sorts, potatoes, mint, parsley, black-currants, gooseberries, peaches, and all the succulent fruits and aromatic herbs of the Rhône valley. Never has the fragrance of basil been so heady.

Scents and smells play a very important part in the life and cooking of Provence. For by the nature of its ingredients, Provençal cuisine is among the most delicate to be found anywhere. The great spreads so typical of French regional cooking are too hearty for the Provençal palate: the traditional cooking of Provence sets out instead to provide subtle delights for all the senses.

'. . . they drank the bottle of wine while a faint wind rocked the pine needles and the sensual heat of early afternoon made blinding freckles on the checkered luncheon cloth.'

F. Scott Fitzgerald, *Tender is the Night*

'*H*aving said that garlic, peppers and aubergines abound in the furrows between the vines, will I have said all? There is also a house . . . but that's less important than that the terrace is covered with wistaria, for example, or that flame-red bignonia and mimosa bushes with big trunks, running from the gate to the front door, honour it with their presence.'

Colette, *Prisons et paradis*

SUMMER

Menu

Green Bean Salad with Pan-fried Sweetbreads

Poached Red Mullet with a Basil Sauce

Pigeons Roasted with Honey

Aubergine Gratin

Strawberry Sorbet

Stuffed Provençale Vegetables

Turbot with Aïoli

Roast Saddle of Rabbit with Basil

Courgette Gratin

Hot Mint Soufflé with Chocolate Sauce

Green Bean Salad with Pan-fried Sweetbreads

SALADE DE HARICOTS VERTS AUX GRILLONS DE
RIS DE VEAU

SERVES 4

4 pairs sweetbreads
(about 600g/1lb 5oz)
sherry vinegar
1 carrot
1 onion
1 leek
20g/²/₃oz/1¹/₂ tbsp unsalted butter
100ml/3¹/₂floz/¹/₂ cup white veal or
chicken stock
100ml/3¹/₂floz/¹/₂ cup white wine
1 bouquet garni
500g/1lb 2oz green beans
1 ripe plum tomato
olive oil
salt and freshly ground black pepper
chives

Preheat the oven to 220°C/425°F/gas mark 7.

TO PREPARE THE SWEETBREADS

Rinse the sweetbreads, then put them in a saucepan of cold water containing a dash of vinegar and heat to boiling point. Remove from the heat immediately and drain, then pull away the filament or skin that encloses them.

Put the sweetbreads in a heavy bottomed saucepan. Peel the carrot and onion and dice them finely with

the leek. Add to the pan with the butter. Fry the sweetbreads and vegetables gently until browned.

Turn the mixture into a baking dish and add the stock, white wine and bouquet garni. Cover and braise in the oven for 15 minutes.

TO COOK THE BEANS

Cook the green beans in boiling salted water until just tender, using plenty of salt, then drain and refresh in cold water so that they stay bright green.

TO MAKE THE SALAD

Skin, seed and juice the tomato and dice the flesh finely. Make a vinaigrette with olive oil, sherry vinegar and seasoning to taste.

Cut the cooked sweetbreads into thin slices. Sauté them in very hot olive oil until well browned and crisp.

Dress the beans with the vinaigrette and arrange on a dish with the tomato. Lay the hot sweetbread slices on top and sprinkle with chopped chives. Serve immediately.

Poached Red Mullet with a Basil Sauce

LE ROUGET POCHÉ À LA NAGE AU BASILIC

SERVES 4

4 red mullet, each weighing 180–200g/6–7oz
4 slices orange
4 slices lemon
4 bay leaves

FOR THE SAUCE

20 basil leaves
5 tarragon leaves
5 sprigs parsley
1 ripe, plum tomato
extra virgin olive oil (preferably from Provence)
a little garlic
3 drops sherry vinegar
salt and freshly ground black pepper

FOR THE NAGE (POACHING LIQUID)

250g/9oz onions
400g/14oz carrots
1 leek (green part only)
150g/5oz celery
1 head garlic
100ml/3½floz/½ cup white wine vinegar
500ml/16floz/2 cups dry white wine
½ lemon
1 sprig thyme
1 bay leaf

TO MAKE THE SAUCE

This should be made the night before and it can be made up to 2 or 3 days in advance since it is essential to blend the flavours. Chop the basil, tarragon, parsley and skinned and seeded tomato finely and put them in the olive oil (we use extra virgin oil made from olives grown in the olive groves below Les Baux). Add a little finely chopped garlic with the vinegar, salt and pepper. Leave to macerate.

TO COOK THE FISH

Prepare the *nage*. Wash all the vegetables and peel if necessary. Slice the onions, carrots and leek in rounds and the celery in matchsticks. Crush the garlic. Put all the ingredients in a large saucepan or fish kettle, add 3 litres/ 5 pints/3 quarts cold water and season with salt and pepper. Bring to the boil and simmer for about 30 minutes.

While the *nage* is cooking, scale the fish but do not gut them (the liver is a delicacy). Place a slice of orange, a slice of lemon and a bay leaf on each fish.

Wrap the fish individually in foil and place them in the *nage*. Cook for about 10 minutes. The fish should still be firm and hold its shape.

Unwrap the fish and arrange on a dish with the orange and lemon slices. Serve the basil sauce separately.

Pigeons Roasted with Honey

PIGEONS AU MIEL

SERVES 4

4 pigeons
2 tsp whole coriander seeds
1 tsp black peppercorns
6 tbsp honey
75g/1½oz/5 tbsp unsalted butter
100ml/3¼floz/½ cup dry white wine
1 tbsp pigeon or chicken stock

Grind the coriander and peppercorns in a pepper mill and stir them into the honey.

Clean and truss the pigeons or ask the butcher to do this.

Melt 20g/⅔oz/4 tsp of the butter in a casserole dish. When it is foaming, brown the pigeons on all sides. This should take about 5 or 6 minutes.

When they are well browned, brush them with honey, coriander and pepper mixture. Cover, reduce the heat and cook, turning them from time to time, for about 30 minutes.

When they are cooked, remove the pigeons from the casserole and keep them warm.

Deglaze the casserole with the white wine.

Add the stock and enrich with the remaining butter. Put the pigeons back in the casserole and simmer a further 2 minutes.

Serve one pigeon per person.

Aubergine Gratin

GRATIN D'AUBERGINES

SERVES 4

4 medium-sized aubergines (eggplants)
200ml/7floz/scant 1 cup olive oil
basil
dry breadcrumbs

FOR THE TOMATO CONCASSÉE

2kg/4½lb ripe plum tomatoes
3 cloves garlic
1 onion
4 tbsp/¼ cup olive oil
1 tbsp tomato paste
1 tbsp sugar
3 sprigs parsley
1 sprig thyme
1 bay leaf
tarragon or basil (optional)
salt and freshly ground black pepper

Select an ovenproof dish or roasting pan large enough to serve as a *bain-marie* for a 25cm/10 inch long gratin dish. Fill the dish with water to a depth of 3cm/1¼ inches and place a sheet of newspaper folded in two in the bottom of the dish or tin to keep the water from boiling during cooking. Place the pan in the oven and preheat it to its highest setting.

TO MAKE THE TOMATO CONCASSÉE

With a small pointed knife, cut out a cone around the stem end of each tomato, removing the little bit of hard flesh that surrounds it. Cut a small cross in the skin at the other end. Plunge the tomatoes into a saucepan of boiling water for 12 seconds, then plunge them into cold water for another 15 seconds. The skin will then come off easily. Cut the tomatoes in half crosswise and remove all the seeds and pulp until only the flesh is left.

Peel the garlic cloves. Peel and chop the onion.

In a large saucepan, brown the whole garlic cloves in the olive oil. Add the chopped onion. Cook very slightly (do not allow them to colour), then add the tomatoes, the tomato paste, sugar, parsley, thyme, bay leaf and, if you are using them, a few tarragon or basil leaves. Season to taste. Leave to simmer gently while you prepare the aubergines.

TO PREPARE THE AUBERGINES

Peel them and cut them lengthwise into slices 3mm/ ⅛ inch thick. In a large frying pan, fry the slices, a few at a time, in the olive oil until well browned on both sides. As the slices are cooked, drain them on absorbent kitchen paper.

TO ASSEMBLE THE GRATIN

Brush the inside of the gratin dish with 1 tsp of olive oil. Cover the bottom with a 5mm/¼ inch layer of tomato *concassée*. Arrange aubergine slices on top and sprinkle with chopped basil. Add a second layer of *concassée* and aubergine, sprinkling again with basil. Finish with a final layer of *concassée* and sprinkle with breadcrumbs.

Place in the oven in the *bain-marie* and cook for 15 minutes. Serve hot.

Strawberry Sorbet

SORBET AUX FRAISES

400g/14oz/2 cups sugar
500g/1lb 2oz ripe strawberries

Place the sugar and 500ml/16fl oz water in a saucepan
and bring to the boil, stirring to dissolve the sugar.
Remove from the heat and put in a cool place.

Crush the strawberries in a blender to yield 500ml/
16fl oz of purée.

Mix the strawberry purée with the sugar syrup and
put into the *sorbetière* (ice cream machine) to freeze.

Serve in glasses decorated with fresh strawberries.

Stuffed Provençale Vegetables

PETITS FARCIS

SERVES 4

2 courgettes (zucchini)
4 medium-sized onions, total weight about
500g/1lb 2oz
4 tomatoes, each with a diameter of 5cm/2 inches
1kg/2¹/₄lb large mushrooms
lemon juice
1 shallot
50g/1³/₄oz/2 tbsp unsalted butter
salt and freshly ground black pepper
chives
freshly grated Parmesan cheese
100g/3¹/₂oz cooked ham
80g/scant 3oz/¹/₃ cup minced (ground) lamb

Slice the courgettes in rounds about 5cm/2 inches thick and peel every other one. Hollow out the centres and set the flesh aside. Cook the shells in boiling salted water until just tender; refresh in cold water and drain.

Peel the onions and cook them in boiling salted water until just tender. Refresh and drain them, then cut the top quarter off each of them. Hollow out the interior of each onion, setting aside two layers. Reserve the onion lids.

Slice the tops off the tomatoes and set the lids aside. Scoop out the flesh and seeds from each tomato and discard it.

Take 4 large mushrooms, remove the stalks carefully and hollow out the caps slightly. Wash them, then rub them with lemon juice to avoid discolouring and put to one side.

With the rest of the mushrooms, make a *duxelles* to serve as a base for the different stuffings: chop the mushrooms and shallot finely and sauté them in the butter, cooking until all the liquid they produce has evaporated. Divide into 4 equal parts.

Preheat the oven to 220°C/425°F/gas mark 7.

To stuff the courgettes, chop the reserved flesh and mix with one portion of *duxelles*, a little salt and pepper and some chopped chives. Stuff each courgette shell with this mixture and sprinkle with Parmesan.

To stuff the onions, chop the reserved hollowed-out layers of onion and mix with one portion of *duxelles*. Season to taste. Fill the hollow onions with this stuffing and replace the lids.

For the mushrooms, mix one portion of *duxelles* with the finely chopped ham. Season to taste. Place

the stuffing in the mushroom caps and sprinkle with Parmesan.

For the tomatoes, sauté the lamb with the last portion of *duxelles* until browned. Season to taste. Put the stuffing in the hollowed tomatoes and replace the lids.

Place the stuffed tomatoes in a shallow oven dish or tray large enough to hold all the vegetables and bake for 15 minutes or until tender and heated through. After about 5 minutes, add the other stuffed vegetables to heat them and to brown the courgettes and mushrooms.

To serve, place one of each vegetable on each plate and pour over a little meat juice from the pan.

Turbot with Aïoli

TURBOT EN BOURRIDE

SERVES 4

1 turbot, weighing 2kg/4½lb
200g/7oz/1 cup garlic
4 egg yolks
salt and freshly ground white pepper
500ml/16floz/2 cups olive oil
2 shallots
250ml/8floz/1 cup white wine
1 litre/1¾ pints/2¾ cups fish stock
4 medium potatoes

Ask the fishmonger to fillet the turbot so that you have 4 equal pieces.

Preheat the oven to 250°C/500°F, or its highest setting.

TO MAKE THE AÏOLI

Peel the garlic and put it through a press or pound it thoroughly in a mortar. Add the egg yolks and a little salt, then dribble in the olive oil slowly, beating all the time, to make a smooth, thick sauce. Set this to one side.

Peel and chop the shallots and put them in a saucepan with the white wine and fish stock. Bring to the boil and reduce by half.

Meanwhile, peel the potatoes and steam or boil them. Keep hot.

Gradually mix the aïoli into the white wine and stock mixture, spoonful by spoonful, until you have a smooth, creamy sauce. Taste and adjust the seasoning. Do not on any account let this sauce boil or it will curdle. Keep the sauce warm.

TO COOK THE FISH

Put the turbot fillets in a baking dish with a little fish stock and cook in the oven for about 3 minutes. Arrange them on individual plates with the sauce and potatoes, and serve immediately.

Roast Saddle of Rabbit with Basil

RÂBLE DE LAPIN RÔTI AU BASILIC

2 rabbits, each weighing 1.2kg/2½lb
1 bunch fresh basil
1 ripe plum tomato
250ml/8floz/1 cup olive oil
½ tsp sherry vinegar
salt and freshly ground black pepper
600g/1¼lb fresh spinach
30g/1oz/2 tbsp unsalted butter

Preheat the oven to 280°C/500°F, or its highest setting.

Chop the basil finely. Skin, seed and juice the tomato and dice the flesh. Mix the basil and tomato with the olive oil and sherry vinegar and season with a little salt. Set aside to macerate.

Cut up the rabbits and take only the two saddles; keep the rest for another dish. Roast the saddles in the hot oven for 12 minutes, then leave them to rest for 10 minutes.

Meanwhile, sauté the spinach in the butter with seasoning to taste and warm the sauce gently until tepid.

To serve, remove the membranes from the rabbit and slice the meat finely. Place some hot spinach in the centre of each plate and arrange the rabbit slices around it. Pour over the tepid sauce and serve immediately.

Courgette Gratin

GRATIN DE COURGETTES

SERVES 4

4 courgettes (zucchini), each about
15cm/6 inches long
10 chives
4 sprigs parsley
100g/3¹/₂oz button mushrooms
25g/³/₄oz/1¹/₂ tbsp unsalted butter
300ml/10floz/1¹/₄ cups crème fraîche
salt and freshly ground black pepper

Select an ovenproof dish or roasting tin large enough to serve as a *bain-marie* for the gratin dish. Fill the dish or tin with water to a depth of 3cm/1¹/₄ inches and place a sheet of newspaper folded in two in the bottom of the dish or tin to keep the water from boiling during cooking. Place the dish or tin in the oven and preheat it to its highest setting.

Peel the courgettes and slice them into rounds 2mm/¹/₈ inch thick. Chop the chives and parsley. Clean the mushrooms and slice them thinly.

Plunge the courgette slices into a saucepan of boiling salted water for 3 minutes. Remove them with

a slotted spoon and drain well. Melt 15g/½oz/1 tbsp of the butter in a frying pan and fry the slices gently until they start to brown. Season with salt and pepper and sprinkle with the chopped chives and parsley.

Meanwhile, fry the mushrooms gently in the remaining butter in another pan until they begin to brown.

Pour the *crème fraîche* into a flameproof gratin dish, put the dish on top of the stove and boil to reduce the *crème fraîche* until it is thick enough to coat the back of a spoon. (There is no risk involved in this: all that will happen is that the *crème fraîche* will thicken – which is what you want it to do.)

Once the *crème fraîche* is reduced, place a layer of half of the courgettes in the gratin dish, followed by a layer of the mushrooms and another layer of the remaining courgettes. Press the vegetables down with a fork as you go so that they are covered by the *crème fraîche*.

Place the gratin dish in the prepared *bain-marie* and cook in the oven for 10 minutes.

Hot Mint Soufflé with Chocolate Sauce

SOUFFLÉ CHAUD À LA MENTHE ET SA SAUCE AU CHOCOLAT

SERVES 6–8

FOR THE MINT SOUFFLÉ

250ml/8floz/1 cup milk
130g/generous 4oz fresh mint leaves
50g/1³/₄oz/¹/₄ cup caster (superfine) sugar
2 egg yolks
50g/1³/₄oz/¹/₃ cup plain (all-purpose) flour
2 tbsp mint syrup
6 egg whites

FOR THE CHOCOLATE SAUCE

100ml/3¹/₄floz/6¹/₂ tbsp milk
100ml/3¹/₄floz/6¹/₂ tbsp crème fraîche
125g/4oz dark plain (semisweet) chocolate
10g/¹/₃oz/2 tbsp butter
2 tbsp mint syrup

TO MAKE THE CRÈME PATISSIÈRE

This may be made several hours ahead or even the day before. Boil the milk and take it off the heat. While it is still boiling hot, add 100g/3¹/₂oz of the mint. Cover

and leave to infuse for at least an hour, then strain through a *chinois* to remove the mint.

Put the sugar in a bowl with the egg yolks. Whisk for a few minutes until the mixture pales. Fold in the flour and mix it in without beating. Bring the mint-flavoured milk to the boil in a heavy-bottomed saucepan and add it to the egg mixture. Pour the mixture back into the saucepan and cook over a low flame, stirring constantly to make sure it does not stick. As soon as it begins to bubble, remove from the heat and leave to cool.

Meanwhile, chop the rest of the mint very finely until you have 3 or 4 tablespoonsful. When the *crème patissière* has cooled completely, fold in the chopped mint and 2 tablespoons of mint syrup. Stir two or three times with a hand whisk to mix well.

TO MAKE THE SOUFFLÉ

This should be made at the last minute, although the egg whites left over from making the *crème patissière* may be kept in the refrigerator until needed. Put them in a bowl and keep them in a cool place, then gradually bring them back to room temperature before beating them.

Preheat the oven to 230°C/450°F/gas mark 8.

The soufflé may be cooked either in one large soufflé dish or in individual ramekins. Butter the dish or ramekins well and roll caster sugar around to coat the sides and bottom evenly, then turn the dish or ramekins over and knock out the excess sugar.

Beat the egg whites until they form stiff peaks. With a spatula, gently fold the *crème patissière* into the egg whites, being careful not to deflate the beaten whites.

Fill the dish or ramekins three-quarters full with the soufflé mixture. Place in the preheated oven and bake for about 12 minutes, or longer for a large soufflé. The soufflé is done when it has risen to one-and-a-half times the height of the uncooked mixture.

TO MAKE THE CHOCOLATE SAUCE

This may be prepared in advance or while the soufflé is cooking. Heat the milk and *crème fraîche* together. Melt the chocolate in the mixture. Add the butter and 2 tablespoons of mint syrup. Mix well and pour into a sauceboat. If the sauce has been prepared in advance, reheat very gently.

TO SERVE

Put some soufflé on each plate and pour the sauce around it. If baked in ramekins, you can make a small hole in the top of each soufflé and spoon in a little sauce. Serve immediately, before the soufflé has time to sink.

'*H*ow can I describe the beauty of the country? Everything is so small, close, exquisite and fertile. Terraced gardens on steep slopes of rich, red earth, orange and lemon trees, olive orchards, tiny pink and peach houses. To Vence – small, on a sun-warmed hill, uncommercial, slow, peaceful. Walked to a Matisse cathedral – small, pure, clean-cut. White, with a blue-tile roof sparkling in the sun.'

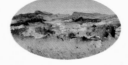

Sylvia Plath, *Postcard to her mother*

'*O* for a draught of vintage! that hath been Cooled a long age in the deep delved earth, Tasting of Flora and the country green, Dance, and Provençal song, and sunburnt mirth!'

John Keats, *Ode to a Nightingale*

$\mathscr{A}$UTUMN

In the vineyards the vines are bowed down under the weight of great bunches of grapes, and in the fields and farmyards the barns are full. Now is the time of the grape harvest, and of the annual pilgrimages to the woods to hunt for cep and chanterelle mushrooms. The last tomatoes, figs and raspberries are gathered in before the first frosts, and the firm, round cabbages are cut.

Now game in all its varieties appears on Provençal tables, accompanied by herbs, picked fresh in summer and dried. A word of warning: intoxicating as they are, thyme, bay, tarragon, and all the other aromatic herbs of Provence should be used sparingly, to enhance and bring out the flavours of a dish. Otherwise, as happens all too often, they may swamp them with their own pungent flavours.

'*S*eptember's spring sees the reflowering of climbing nasturtiums, roses, the tireless multicoloured purslane and little rambling petunias.'

Colette, *Belles Saisons*

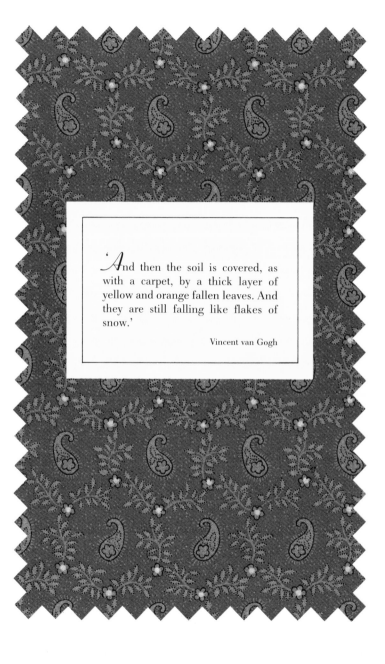

'And then the soil is covered, as with a carpet, by a thick layer of yellow and orange fallen leaves. And they are still falling like flakes of snow.'

Vincent van Gogh

$\mathcal{A}$UTUMN

Menu

Lamb Terrine with a Red Pepper Sauce

Seabass in a Sea-salt Crust with Tarragon Sauce

Chicken Sautéed with Young Garlic

Artichoke Mousse

Nougat Parfait with a Raspberry Sauce

Scrambled Eggs with Sea Urchins and Caviar

Fillets of Sole with a Saffron Sauce

Noisettes of Lamb with Olives

Green Cabbage with Tarragon

Orange Tart

Lamb Terrine with a Red Pepper Sauce

CHARLOTTE D'AGNEAU AU COULIS DE POIVRONS ROUGE

SERVES 8

500g/1lb 2oz boned shoulder of lamb
4 ripe plum tomatoes
1 onion
olive oil
1 tsp sugar
salt and freshly ground black pepper
30g/1oz/2 tbsp unsalted butter
200g/7oz aubergines (eggplants)
2 tsp chopped parsley
1 small clove garlic
1 egg yolk

FOR THE SAUCE

250g/9oz sweet red peppers
40g/1½oz/3 tbsp unsalted butter
250ml/8fl oz/1 cup crème fraîche

Preheat the oven to 250°C/475°F/gas mark 9.

TO MAKE THE SAUCE

Cut the sweet peppers in half and remove the core and seeds. Cut them into thin strips. Put them in a roasting dish with the butter and cook in the oven for 10 minutes. Add the *crème fraîche* and cook for a further 5 minutes. Put the mixture in a blender and purée until smooth. Taste and season if necessary. Sieve through a muslin or cheesecloth *chinois* and leave to cool.

Skin and seed the tomatoes and chop into a pulp. Peel and finely chop the onion.

Put 4 tbsp olive oil in a sauté pan with the tomatoes, onion, sugar and salt and pepper to taste. Cook over a medium heat, stirring frequently, until you have a rather liquid purée. Set aside.

Cut the lamb into pieces as if for kebabs. Put the butter and 1 tsp olive oil in a flameproof casserole over a high heat. Add the lamb pieces and cook for 2–3 minutes, until browned all over but still pink inside. Remove from the casserole and leave to cool, then with a knife or in a blender, cut them into very small pieces but do not mince (grind).

Cut the aubergines into slices about 2mm/⅛ inch thick, then fry them in a sauté pan in 4 tbsp olive oil until lightly browned on both sides.

Remove one quarter of the aubergine slices and set aside.

To the sauté pan, add the tomato mixture, the chopped parsley, the finely chopped garlic and the lamb. Cook until excess liquid has evaporated.

Remove from the heat and leave to cool. When the mixture is lukewarm, add the egg yolk to bind it and mix well.

Butter 8 ramekins. Line the bottoms and sides with the reserved aubergine slices, then fill them with the lamb mixture. Cover the ramekins with foil and put them in a *bain-marie* (see page 14). Cook in a preheated 120°C/250°F/gas mark ½ oven for 10 minutes.

Remove from the oven and unmould when cool.

Seabass in a Sea-salt Crust with Tarragon Sauce

LOUP EN CROÛTE DE SEL, SAUCE ESTRAGON

SERVES 4

1 seabass, weighing 1.2kg/2½lb
2kg/4½lb coarse sea salt
300g/10oz/2 cups plain (all-purpose) flour

FOR THE STOCK

1.5kg/3¼lb fish heads and bones from sole,
whiting, etc.; avoid oily fish such as salmon and red mullet
1 shallot
1 large onion
1 stalk celery
8 sprigs parsley
2 tbsp olive oil

FOR THE SAUCE

1 shallot
100ml/3½floz white wine
200ml/7floz/scant 1 cup crème fraîche
10 tarragon leaves
salt and freshly ground black pepper

Preheat the oven to 230°C/450°F/gas mark 8.

Gut the fish and remove the dorsal fin. Do not scale it, as the scales protect it during cooking and make it easier to remove the skin afterwards.

Soak the fish heads and bones in cold running water for 15 minutes so that they do not impart too strong a flavour to the stock. Peel and chop the shallot, peel and finely slice the onion, and slice the celery. Chop the parsley finely.

Put the bones and fish heads, onion, shallot and celery in a sauté pan with the olive oil and fry gently for 5 minutes to draw out their juices. Add 1.5 litres/ 2½ pints/1½ quarts of cold water and the parsley, and simmer for 20 minutes, skimming off the froth regularly. Strain through a *chinois*. Set aside 200ml/ 7fl oz/scant 1 cup, and freeze the rest in small quantities for other recipes.

TO COOK THE FISH

Mix together the coarse salt, flour and 200 ml/7fl oz/ scant 1 cup water, or enough to make a paste. Smear the fish with the paste to cover completely and cook in the oven for 20–25 minutes.

TO MAKE THE SAUCE

This can be made while the fish is cooking. Peel and chop the shallot and put it in a saucepan with the white wine and reserved stock. Boil to reduce by half. Whisk in the *crème fraîche* and add the tarragon. Continue reducing until the sauce is smooth and creamy. Season to taste. Strain through a *chinois* and keep warm, stirring occasionally.

TO SERVE

Break the salt crust, remove the skin and place the fish on a serving dish. Serve the sauce separately.

Chicken Sautéed with Young Garlic

POULET SAUTÉ À L'AIL NOUVEAU

SERVES 4

1 free-range chicken, about 1.8kg/4lb
2 heads new, young garlic
300ml/½ pint goose fat
1 onion
5 ripe plum tomatoes
30g/1oz/2 tbsp unsalted butter
1 wineglass white wine
500ml/16floz/2 cups chicken stock
2 sprigs thyme
salt and freshly ground black pepper

TO PREPARE THE GARLIC

This can be done in advance. Peel the cloves and poach them in simmering water for 2 minutes. Drain, then cook in the goose fat over a low heat for 15 minutes.

TO COOK THE CHICKEN

Cut up the chicken and chop each piece, legs, wings, breast, etc., into 2 or 3 smaller pieces.

Peel the onion and slice into rings. Skin, juice, seed and dice the tomatoes.

Put the chicken pieces in a sauté pan with two-thirds of the butter and cook over a medium heat, turning, until they are a light golden yellow on all sides.

In another pan, fry the onion gently in the rest of the butter. Add the chopped tomatoes and pour this mixture over the chicken pieces. Moisten with the white wine and stock. Add the thyme and leave to cook, half-covered, for 30 minutes.

Add the drained garlic and simmer for 5 minutes so that its flavour impregnates the sauce. Season to taste and serve hot.

Artichoke Mousse

MOUSSELINE D'ARTICHAUTS

SERVES 4

16 small or 8 medium-size globe
artichokes
juice of 1 lemon
1 tbsp plain (all-purpose) flour
500ml/16floz/2 cups crème fraîche
10g/¹/₃oz/2 tsp unsalted butter
50ml/3¹/₂ tbsp truffle juice
salt and freshly ground white pepper

Prepare the artichokes by cutting away the leaves with scissors until only the hearts (*fonds*) are left. Scrape away the hairy chokes. As each artichoke is prepared, put it into a saucepan of salted water to which the lemon juice and flour have been added. This will stop them from discolouring. Simmer them in this mixture until they are cooked (about 40 minutes), then drain them well before passing them through a fine sieve into a clean saucepan.

Add the *crème fraîche*, butter and truffle juice to the puréed artichoke hearts, keeping the saucepan on the heat and stirring vigorously all the while with a hand whisk, or preferably a wooden spatula. The texture should be smooth and creamy without being too liquid.

Season to taste with salt and freshly ground white pepper, and serve hot.

Nougat Parfait with a Raspberry Sauce

NOUGAT GLACÉ ET SON COULIS DE FRAMBOISES

SERVES 6

FOR THE NOUGATINE

160g/5¹/₂oz/1 cup blanched almonds
220g/8oz/1 cup sugar

FOR THE RASPBERRY SAUCE

500g/1lb 2oz/2 pints raspberries
150g/5oz/²/₃ cup caster (superfine) sugar

FOR THE NOUGAT

4 egg whites
250g/9oz/1¹/₄ cups sugar
500ml/16floz/2 cups crème fraîche
250g/9oz mixed glacé fruits

TO MAKE THE NOUGATINE

Make this the day before. Toast the almonds gently in a moderate oven for about 5 minutes, stirring occasionally to make sure they do not burn.

Put the sugar in a saucepan over a high heat and stir constantly with a wooden spatula until it melts and then turns the colour of caramel.

Stir in the toasted almonds and mix well. Pour the mixture on to a tray or baking sheet, spreading it evenly and not too quickly. When it has cooled thoroughly and set, use a knife to chop it into slivers.

TO MAKE THE RASPBERRY SAUCE

This, too, may be made in advance. The proportions given in the ingredients may be doubled and strawberries may be used instead of raspberries.

Wash the fruit and put it in a blender with the sugar. Purée until smooth. Sieve to remove the raspberry seeds. This sauce can be kept in the refrigerator for several days, and it also freezes well.

TO MAKE THE ICED NOUGAT

Beat the egg whites until they form very stiff peaks. Whites that have been separated for some hours, or even days, are easier to beat and will hold their shape better.

Put the sugar in a saucepan with 600ml/1 pint/2½ cups water over a medium heat and heat, stirring, to

dissolve the sugar. Then boil until the syrup reaches the soft ball stage (that is, when a little of the syrup dropped into a bowl of cold water forms a soft ball) or registers 117°C/240°F on a sugar (candy) thermometer.

Remove the syrup from the heat at once and pour it on to the whisked egg whites, beating well to make a sort of meringue mixture. Leave to cool.

Whip the *crème fraîche* until it is thick but not stiff (in warm weather be careful to keep it cool, otherwise it will turn into butter). Add the meringue, chopped glacé fruits and nougatine and mix well. Pour into individual ramekins. Cover and freeze for at least 2 hours.

TO SERVE

Unmould immediately before serving. Pour a little raspberry sauce into each dish and place the nougat parfait in the middle. Garnish each serving with a raspberry or a mint leaf.

Scrambled Eggs with Sea Urchins and Caviar

OEUFS BROUILLÉS AU CAVIAR D'OURSINS

SERVES 2

50g/scant 2oz/4 tbsp unsalted butter
6 eggs
12 sea urchins, coral only
salt and freshly ground black pepper
2 tbsp double (heavy) cream
2 tbsp whipped cream
2 tbsp truffle juice
2 tsp caviar
puff pastry strips formed into two small latticework squares for garnish

Heat the butter gently in a heavy-bottomed sauté pan. Beat the eggs with the sea urchin coral as if for an omelette and season. Add this mixture to the pan and cook over a low heat, stirring constantly with a wooden spatula.

When the mixture reaches a creamy consistency, fold in the double cream. Check the seasoning and transfer into a small serving dish.

Lightly mix the whipped cream with the truffle juice. Stir in the caviar and pour over the scrambled eggs. Garnish with the pastry latticework.

Serve without delay, as the eggs will continue to cook even after they have been removed from the heat.

Fillets of Sole with a Saffron Sauce

PETITE NAGE DE SOLES AU SAFRAN

SERVES 4

16 fillets of sole
2 carrots
2 courgettes (zucchini)
160g/5oz/10 tbsp unsalted butter
a pinch of saffron
fish stock (see page 71)

TO MAKE THE VEGETABLES

Peel the carrots and make grooves along their length using a cannelle knife, then slice them in rounds and steam or boil them. Set aside.

Peel the courgettes and slice them into lengths of 3 or 4cm/1¼ or 1½ inches. Cut each piece in four lengthwise, and with a small sharp knife trim the edges to make oval or barrel shapes. Steam or boil. Set aside.

TO MAKE THE FILLETS OF SOLE

Cut the fillets into *gougeonettes*: tiny strips each of 7 or 8cm/3 or 3¼ inches long.

Bring the stock to the boil with the saffron and add the fish. Cook the *gougeonettes* for about 2 minutes, then remove them with a slotted spoon and put them to one side in a warmed dish covered with foil.

TO MAKE THE SAUCE

Increase the heat under the stock and boil to reduce by a third, until there is about 500ml/16fl oz/2 cups left. Reduce the heat to very low and, whisking the stock, add the butter, kneaded until it is soft, little by little. Add the *gougeonettes* to the sauce and reheat briefly.

TO SERVE

Arrange the *gougeonettes*, carrots and courgettes on the plates and pour the sauce over.

Noisettes of Lamb with Olives

NOISETTES D'AGNEAU AUX OLIVES

SERVES 2

1 loin of lamb, with 8 chop bones
2 lambs' brains
1 lamb's foot
1 litre/1¼ pints/1 quart white veal or
chicken stock
1 ripe, plum tomato
80g/scant 3oz/5½ tbsp unsalted butter
flour for coating
2 shallots
chives
salt and freshly ground black pepper
10 black olives, sliced
200g/7oz hot, freshly cooked broccoli

FOR THE STOCK

20g/²/₃oz/4 tsp unsalted butter
1 onion
1 carrot
1 leek
1 stalk celery
50ml/3½ tbsp white wine
1 litre/1¼ pints/1 quart water
thyme
1 bay leaf

1 tbsp tapenade
1 egg yolk
2 egg whites

Bone the loin of lamb and trim it to make a neat shape (or ask your butcher to do this for you). Keep the bones and trimmings.

TO MAKE THE STOCK

In a large saucepan, brown the lamb bones and trimmings in the butter, then add the peeled and diced onion, carrot, leek and celery and let them sweat for about 5 minutes. Deglaze the pan with the white wine, then add the water, the thyme and bay leaf. Simmer, skimming the fat from time to time, until you have a reduced, well-flavoured stock, about 30–45 minutes. Strain and set aside. (You will need only a few spoonfuls of stock for this dish; keep the remainder for other recipes).

TO MAKE THE LAMB

Soak the brains and lamb's foot in cold water for several hours, then drain and remove the filaments surrounding the brains. Cook the brains and foot in the white veal or chicken stock for 10 minutes. Drain and set the brains aside. When cool, remove the meat from the foot and dice it. Set aside.

Peel, seed and juice the tomato, then dice the flesh. Set aside.

Preheat the oven to 200°C/400°F/gas mark 6.

Melt 10g/⅓oz/2 tsp of the butter in a sauté pan over a high heat. Seal the lamb for 1 minute on all sides, then put it in the oven and cook for a further 5 minutes. Remove from the heat and leave to rest for 5 minutes.

Roll the brains in flour, shake off the excess and fry in 20g/²⁄₃oz/4 tsp of the butter over a high heat until crisp on the outside.

In another pan, cook the peeled and finely chopped shallots, diced lamb's foot and tomato with 20g/²⁄₃oz/ 4 tsp of the butter until heated through. Season with chopped chives, salt and pepper.

TO MAKE THE OLIVE SOUFFLÉS

While the lamb is cooking, mix the *tapenade* with the egg yolk. Beat the whites until they form stiff peaks and fold in the *tapenade* mixture. Put into 2 small buttered individual moulds that are about 1cm/½ inch deep and bake in the oven for 3 minutes.

TO SERVE

Carve the loin of lamb into 8 noisettes, and arrange them on 2 hot plates in a semi-circle on a bed of the diced lamb mixture. Unmould the little olive soufflés and arrange the brains on top. Enrich a few spoonfuls of the reheated stock with the remaining butter and pour over the noisettes, then garnish with the sliced olives. Glaze the hot broccoli with a little extra butter and arrange it around the edge of the dish. Serve immediately.

Green Cabbage with Tarragon

CHOU VERT À L'ESTRAGON

SERVES 4

1 savoy cabbage
3 sprigs tarragon
30g/1oz/2 tbsp butter
salt

With a small, pointed knife, cut diagonally around the stem of the cabbage to remove the core. Discard the outermost leaves. Wash the cabbage in cold water.

Blanch the cabbage in boiling salted water for 3 minutes. Drain, refresh in cold water and drain again.

Cut the cabbage into fine strips, 5mm/¼ inch wide. Sauté the strips in the butter until tender. Add the tarragon leaves and salt to taste, and serve.

Orange Tart

TARTE À L'ORANGE 'BAUMANIÈRE'

SERVES 4–6

FOR THE FILLING

60g/2oz/4 tbsp unsalted butter
grated zest of 1 orange
100ml/3¹/₂fl oz/¹/₂ cup orange juice
6 eggs
200g/7oz/1 cup sugar

FOR THE PÂTE SABLÉE

150g/5oz/2¹/₂ cups unsalted butter
250g/9oz/1³/₄ cups plain (all-purpose) flour
30g/1oz/¹/₃ cup ground almonds
90g/3oz/6 tbsp caster (superfine) sugar
1 egg

Preheat the oven to 180°C/350°F/gas mark 4.

Melt the butter with the orange zest and juice over a low heat.

Beat the eggs and sugar together in a bowl with quick, light movements until light and fluffy.

When the butter has melted, bring the mixture to the boil. Remove from the heat and fold in the egg and sugar mixture. Blend together well with a whisk, then return to the heat. Bring to the boil over a medium flame, taking care that it does not stick.

As soon as the mixture begins to boil (when the first big bubbles appear), remove from the heat. Pour into a bowl and leave to cool completely.

Beat the butter until it is soft. Rub together the butter, flour, ground almonds and 30g/1oz/⅓ cup of the sugar, working quickly and lightly.

Add the remaining sugar and the egg and mix together lightly, just until the ingredients form a paste. If the rubbing or mixing is too heavy-handed, the pastry will not have the right consistency.

Roll out the pastry, preferably on a cool marble slab and use to line a 20cm/8 inch flan ring on a baking sheet or a springform loose-bottomed tart tin. Bake blind (empty) in the preheated oven for 20 minutes, until the pastry begins to brown. Take out of the oven. Remove the pastry case from the ring or tin and leave to cool on a wire rack, so that the bottom dries out and becomes crispy.

When both filling and case are quite cool, fill the pastry case with the orange cream.

'. . . and as I went on it seemed that true happiness would consist in wandering through such a land on foot, on September afternoons, when one might stretch one's self on the warm ground in some shady hollow and listen to the hum of bees and the whistle of melancholy shepherds. . . . It was a pleasure to be in Provence again – a land where the silver grey earth is impregnated with the light of the sky.'

Henry James, *A Little Tour in France*

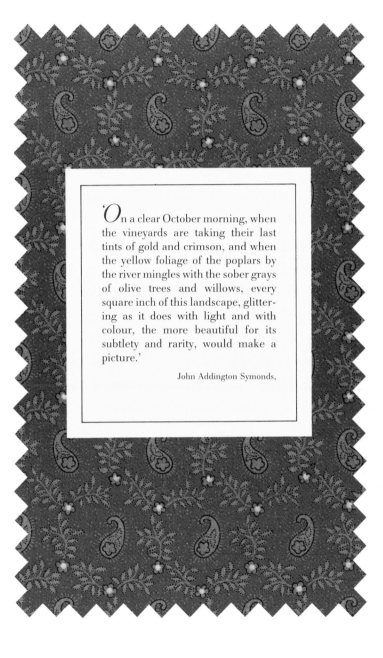

'On a clear October morning, when the vineyards are taking their last tints of gold and crimson, and when the yellow foliage of the poplars by the river mingles with the sober grays of olive trees and willows, every square inch of this landscape, glittering as it does with light and with colour, the more beautiful for its subtlety and rarity, would make a picture.'

John Addington Symonds,

Winter

Winter is a time of rest for gardeners, but not everything in the kitchen garden is dormant: some hardy vegetables are able to adapt to the rigours of the season.

Nature is less generous now, and cooking requires a little more imagination. Now is the season of lentils, fennel, lamb's lettuce, chestnuts, oranges and other citrus fruits; but above all it is the time for truffles, those magical truffles that we are lucky enough to have available in plenty from the Tricastin, at the southern end of the Rhône valley.

'The inn's table groans with mar-
zipan cakes, crystallized fruits,
Provençale sweetmeats sugared and
sugared again; a bah-ahing outside
tells us Midnight Mass has just
finished and that the shepherds are
bringing their lambs back, blessed
beneath their capes.'

Colette, *Belles Saisons I*

'*L*ucky Midi. It has, from January, daffodils, almonds, mimosa in great yellow clouds, pinks, anemones, while the rest of France is stiff with cold.'

Colette, *Belles Saisons I*

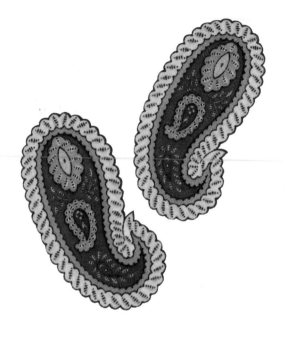

WINTER

Menu

Truffle Salad

Fillets of Sea Bream with a Rosemary Sauce

Salmi of Wild Duck

Celeriac Purée

Spiced Pear Tarts

Mussel Soup

Roast Monkfish Tail

Fillet of Beef 'Baumanière'

Potato Purée with Olive Oil

Chocolate Gâteau 'l'Ardéchois'

Truffle Salad

PETITE SALADE DE TRUFFES GOURMANDE

SERVES 2

80g/2¹/₂oz fresh truffles
1 tbsp sherry vinegar
3 tbsp olive oil
dash of lemon juice
salt and freshly ground black pepper
200g/7oz lamb's lettuce

Slice the truffle or truffles in very thin rounds.

Make a vinaigrette with the sherry vinegar and olive oil. Add a dash of lemon juice and salt and pepper to taste.

Wash and dry the lamb's lettuce. Put it in a salad bowl with half the vinaigrette and toss well.

TO SERVE

Arrange a little lamb's lettuce on each plate with a slice of truffle on top. Pour a little vinaigrette on to each slice of truffle.

Fillets of Sea Bream with a Rosemary Sauce

DORADE ROYALE À LA CRÈME DE ROMARIN

SERVES 4

1 sea bream (red porgy) or sea bass,
weighing about 2kg/4¹/₂lb
10g/¹/₃oz/about 2 tbsp dried rosemary
200ml/7floz/scant 1 cup fish stock
(see page 71)
500ml/16floz/2 cups crème fraîche
nage for poaching (see page 43)
salt and freshly ground black pepper

Ask the fishmonger to fillet the fish and cut it into four equal pieces.

Heat the rosemary in the fish stock so as to flavour it (do not be tempted to use too much rosemary: the flavour should remain subtle so that it does not overwhelm the fish). Add the *crème fraîche* and boil to reduce until the sauce will just coat a spoon. Strain through a *chinois*. Keep warm.

Steam the pieces of fish, in a basket, in the *nage* until cooked (about 3 minutes). Season.

Arrange each fillet on a plate and coat with the sauce.

Salmi of Wild Duck

SALMIS DE CANARDS SAUVAGES

SERVES 4

2 oven-ready wild ducks
salt and freshly ground black pepper
1 carrot
1 onion
2 shallots
60g/2oz/4 tbsp unsalted butter
2 tbsp oil
250ml/8floz/1 cup dry white wine
120ml/4floz/¹/₂ cup Madeira
1 sprig thyme
1 bay leaf
30g/1oz/3 tbsp plain (all-purpose) flour

Remove the giblets from the ducks. Season the cavities with salt and pepper and truss the birds. Chop the livers.

Peel and finely slice the carrot; peel and chop the onion and shallots. Set aside.

Heat 30g/1oz/2 tbsp of the butter and the oil in a cast-iron casserole and cook the ducks for 20 minutes over a medium heat, turning from time to time to make sure they are well browned on all sides.

Remove the ducks and cut off the breasts and legs, which should still be pink in the middle. Keep them warm in a dish covered with foil in a low oven (60°C/140°F/gas mark 1).

On a chopping board, chop the duck carcasses roughly. Put them back into the casserole with the onion, carrot and shallots and cook for 5 minutes.

Add the white wine, Madeira and 250ml/8floz water to deglaze the pan, if necessary scraping the sides and bottom with a wooden spatula to pick up all the caramelized juices. Add the thyme and bay leaf and boil to reduce over a high heat for 30 minutes.

Meanwhile, prepare some *beurre manié* by working together the remaining butter and the flour to make a paste.

Thicken the sauce by gradually adding the *beurre manié* and the chopped livers.

Cook the sauce for another 10 minutes then sieve through a *chinois* (strainer) and return to the casserole. Add the duck breasts and legs and simmer gently for 5 minutes, to heat them through.

Celeriac Purée

SERVES 4

300g/10oz celeriac (celery root)
250g/9oz potatoes
40g/1½oz/3 tbsp unsalted butter
300ml/10floz/1¼ cups crème fraîche
salt and freshly ground white pepper

Peel the celeriac and potatoes and cut into quarters.

Cook the celeriac in boiling salted water for 20 minutes, then add the potatoes and boil for a further 20 minutes.

Drain, then purée in a moulinette or blender. Fold in the butter and *crème fraîche* and beat well with a whisk until the purée is light and smooth. Season to taste and reheat briefly before serving.

Spiced Pear Tarts

TARTES AUX POIRES ET AUX EPICES CARAMELISÉES

MAKES 10 TARTLETS

FOR THE PEARS

1 kg 200g/2lb 11oz/6 cups sugar
10ml/2 tsp grated nutmeg
6–8 cloves
20ml/4 tsp ground ginger
small cinnamon stick
pared strip of lemon zest
$^1/_2$ vanilla pod
2kg/4$^1/_2$lb pears
icing (confectioners') sugar

FOR THE PASTRY

225g/8oz/2 sticks unsalted butter
225g/8oz/1 cup caster (superfine) sugar
150g/5oz/1$^2/_3$ cups ground hazelnuts
225g/8oz/1$^2/_3$ cups plain (all-purpose) flour
2 tsp baking powder
6 size 3/US large eggs
finely grated zest of 1 lemon
2 tsp ground allspice
1 tsp vanilla essence (extract)
$^3/_4$ tsp salt

FOR THE CARAMEL SAUCE

250g/9oz/1$^1/_4$ cups sugar
500ml/16floz/2 cups crème fraîche

TO MAKE THE PEARS

Make a syrup with 1kg/2$^1/_4$lb/5 cups of the sugar and
2–3 litres/3$^1/_2$–5 pints/2–3 quarts of water. Melt the
remaining sugar in another pan and cook to a golden

caramel, then add it to the syrup to colour it. Add the nutmeg, cloves, ginger, cinnamon, lemon zest and vanilla.

Peel the pears and core them from the base using an apple corer. Poach the pears in the syrup for about 15 minutes, until they are cooked but still firm. Leave them to cool in the syrup.

TO MAKE THE PASTRY

Preheat the oven to 180°C/350°F/gas mark 4.

Cream the butter with the sugar, then work in the rest of the ingredients in the order listed. Roll out and use to line tartlet tins, each about 10cm/4 inches in diameter. Bake for about 15 minutes.

TO MAKE THE CARAMEL SAUCE

Put the sugar in the saucepan and cook over a moderate heat until the sugar melts and turns to a brown caramel. Heat the *crème fraîche* until it boils, then pour it over the caramel, stirring well. Keep warm.

Take each pear and, holding it at the top and starting one third of the way down, make vertical cuts all around, 2mm/⅛ inch apart. Place each pear in a pastry case. Sprinkle with icing sugar and caramelize under the grill (broiler).

Serve immediately, with the hot caramel sauce.

Mussel Soup

SOUPE DE MOULES

SERVES 4

1kg/2¹/₄lb mussels
100ml/3¹/₂floz/¹/₂ cup white wine
3 ripe plum tomatoes
1 onion
1 leek
1 carrot
50ml/3¹/₂ tbsp olive oil
1 clove garlic
1 bouquet garni
500ml/16floz/2 cups fish stock (see page 71)
200ml/7floz/scant 1 cup crème fraîche
10g/¹/₃oz/about 4 tsp saffron powder
salt and freshly ground black pepper
1 sprig fresh thyme

Discard any mussels that are not firmly closed or that feel lighter than the rest. If the mussels have not been cleaned, scrub them under cold running water and scrape off the 'beards' with a small knife.

Put the mussels in a large saucepan and pour over the white wine. Cover and cook for about 3 minutes, stirring from time to time. Leave to cool, then remove the mussels from their shells. Strain the liquor through a *chinois*.

Skin, seed and juice the tomatoes and dice the flesh finely.

Make a *mirepoix* with the onion, leek and carrot: peel them, then dice them finely and put them in a pan with the olive oil. Cover the pan and sweat the vegetables gently, without colouring, for 5–7 minutes.

Add the peeled and crushed garlic, tomatoes and bouquet garni to the *mirepoix*, followed by the mussel

liquor and fish stock and simmer for about 30 minutes.

Add the *crème fraîche* and the saffron. Boil to reduce to a creamy consistency. Check the seasoning. Discard the bouquet garni.

Put the mussels and a few leaves of thyme in the soup plates and ladle the soup over.

Roast Monkfish Tail

QUEUE DE LOTTE RÔTIE AU FOUR

SERVES 4

800g/1¾lb monkfish tail
2 cloves garlic
100g/3½oz/1½ cups parsley
120ml/4floz/½ cup olive oil
juice of ½ lemon

Ask the fishmonger to skin the monkfish tail.

Preheat the oven to 250°C/500°F or its highest setting.

Peel the garlic cloves and remove the central 'germ'. Chop the garlic and parsley finely and mix them together.

Place the monkfish in a roasting dish and sprinkle with the olive oil and lemon juice.

Roast in the oven for 20 minutes, basting from time to time with the cooking juices.

As soon as the fish is cooked, place it on a serving dish, pour the cooking juices over and sprinkle with the chopped garlic and parsley.

Fillet of Beef 'Baumanière'

FILET DE BOEUF 'BAUMANIÈRE'

SERVES 4–6

1 carrot
1 shallot
1 onion
1 bottle Côtes du Rhône (or similar dry
French red wine)
2 chicken livers
6 anchovy fillets in olive oil, crushed
1kg/2lb fillet of beef (beef tenderloin roast)
olive oil
50g/scant 2oz/4 tbsp unsalted butter
salt and freshly ground black pepper

Preparation of the sauce should be started a day in advance to give the subtle flavours – especially that of the anchovies – time to develop and mature.

Peel the carrot, shallot and onion and cut into small dice. Put them in a saucepan with the red wine over a medium heat.

Boil to reduce for 30 minutes, then thicken the sauce with the chicken livers, chopped. Add the crushed anchovy fillets and reduce for another few minutes, then sieve through a *chinois* (strainer). Leave to rest for 24 hours.

The following day, return the sauce to the heat and reduce it until it starts to really thicken (at this stage it should just cover the bottom of the pan). Be careful not to let it stick: stir it frequently with a wooden spatula.

Brush the meat with olive oil, then sauté it in more olive oil, cooking it well or lightly according to taste.

Meanwhile, finish off the sauce by enriching it with the butter. Gradually add small pieces of softened butter, whisking all the while with a sauce whisk.

Cut the meat in thick slices, season to taste, pour the sauce over and serve very hot.

Potato Purée with Olive Oil

PURÉE À L'HUILE D'OLIVE DE POMMES DE TERRE

SERVES 4

800g/1¾lb baking potatoes
50g/1¾oz/2 tbsp unsalted butter
200ml/7fl oz/scant 1 cup hot crème fraîche
100ml/3½fl oz/½ cup extra virgin olive oil
salt

Peel the potatoes and cut them in quarters. Rinse and cook in boiling salted water.

When they are cooked, drain them well and sieve, mash or blend them to a purée.

Add the butter and beat with a wooden spoon until smooth. Stir in the hot *crème fraîche* and olive oil, season with salt and serve immediately.

Chocolate Gâteau 'l'Ardéchois'

GÂTEAU AU CHOCOLAT 'L'ARDÉCHOIS'

SERVES 6–8

FOR THE GÉNOISE

3 eggs
85g/2³/₄oz/6 tbsp caster (superfine) sugar
10g/¹/₃oz/2 tsp unsalted butter
85g/2³/₄oz/¹/₂ cup plain (all-purpose) flour

FOR THE MERINGUE

2 egg whites
125g/4oz/³/₄ cup caster (superfine) sugar

FOR THE SYRUP

120g/4oz/³/₄ cup sugar
800ml/1¹/₃ pints/3¹/₄ cups water

FOR THE GANACHE

125ml/4floz crème fraîche
150g/5oz dark plain (semisweet) chocolate
1 500g/1lb 2oz can unsweetened chestnut purée

Preheat the oven to 180°C/350°F/gas mark 4.

TO MAKE THE GÉNOISE

Put the eggs and sugar in a *bain-marie* (see page 14),
or a double boiler and blend gently with a hand whisk
for about 1 minute, until the mixture is tepid. Remove
from the heat and beat with an electric mixer until the

mixture is very thick and creamy and forms a 'ribbon' when a spatula is plunged into the mixture and lifted out again. Fold in the melted butter and flour and blend well together.

Butter a 20–23cm/8–9 inch round cake tin and pour in the mixture (it should not come more than halfway up the sides of the tin as it will rise during cooking). Put into the oven to bake for 30 minutes.

When the *génoise* has thoroughly cooled, split it horizontally into three rounds of equal thickness.

TO MAKE THE MERINGUE

In a *bain-marie* or a double boiler placed in a pan of gently simmering water, stir together the egg whites and sugar for 2 minutes. Remove from the heat and beat the mixture until it forms stiff peaks. Place a sheet of buttered greaseproof (waxed) paper or parchment paper on a baking sheet, spread the meringue in two rounds of equal diameter to the *génoise*. Dry out in a very cool oven (about 80°C/175°F) for 30 minutes. Check that the meringue is thoroughly cooked before removing from the oven.

TO MAKE THE SYRUP

Put the sugar and water in a saucepan and bring to the boil. Boil for 1 minute. Remove from heat and leave to cool.

TO MAKE THE GANACHE

In a small saucepan, bring the *crème fraîche* to the boil, then add the chocolate broken into small pieces. When the chocolate has completely melted, leave the mixture to cool so that it starts to set.

When the *ganache* has reached the consistency of clotted or very thick cream, start to assemble the gâteau.

TO ASSEMBLE THE GÂTEAU

Place a round of génoise on the serving plate. Pour a little of the syrup over it, just enough to moisten – not too much or the gâteau may sink. Spread with a layer of *ganache*, then place a meringue round on top and cover it with a layer of chestnut purée. Then repeat: *génoise*, syrup, *ganache*, meringue, chestnut purée. Finish with the last round of *génoise*. The second and third rounds of *génoise* can be moistened with syrup on both sides.

Smooth the remaining *ganache* over the top and sides of the gateau, then roughen the surface into little peaks.

'*M*eanwhile . . . the familiar prospects of vines, olives, cypresses welcome one – either trussed back by the winter gales in glittering silver-green bundles, or softly powdered by the gold dust of the summers, blown from the threshing floor by the freshets of sea-winds. Yes, the great wines of the south sleep softly on in the French earth like a pledge that the enchanted landscapes of the European heart will always exist, will never fade against this taut wind-haunted blue sky where the mistral rumbles and screams all winter long.'

Lawrence Durrell, *Spirit of Place*

'*I* could see [the herbs] and breathe their delicate smell; and I'd say their names just for myself, just for me who had collected them during the summer. . . . For I had no other happiness than to live, hidden from the world, in this attic, among the plants and flowers of the fields.'

Henri Bosco, *Le Mas Theotime*

ACKNOWLEDGEMENTS

The author and publishers would like to thank Souleiado for the use of the fabrics throughout the book, 'Dessin Souleiado' copyright CH. DEMERY SA., and the following copyright holders for their permission to reproduce the following: the extract from *The Unquiet Grave* by Cyril Connolly is reprinted by permission of Hamish Hamilton Ltd; the extract 'Que ma joie demeure' from *Joy of Man's Desiring* by Jean Giono copyright © 1940 by Katherine Allen Clarke published by North Point Press; the extracts from *Bella-Vista* and *Prisons et Paradis* by Colette are reprinted by permission of Fayard, Paris; the extract from *Le Jardin d'Hyacinthe* by Henri Bosco copyright © 1946 Editions Gallimard; 'Postcard to her Mother' from *Letters Home By Sylvia Plath: Correspondence 1950–1963* by Sylvia Plath, copyright © 1975 by Aurelia Schober Plath is reprinted by permission of Faber and Faber Ltd., London and Harper and Row, Publishers, Inc., New York; the extract from *Tender is the Night* by F. Scott Fitzgerald is reprinted by permission of The Bodley Head, London and the Estate of F. Scott Fitzgerald; the extracts from *Belles Saisons I* by Colette are reprinted by permission of Flammarion, Paris; the Vincent van Gogh translation is reprinted by permission of Julian More; the extract 'Across Secret Provence' from *Spirit of Place* by Lawrence Durrell is reprinted by permission of Faber and Faber Ltd., London and Curtis Brown, London on behalf of the author © Lawrence Durrell; the extract from *Le Mas Theotime* by Henri Bosco copyright © 1952 Editions Gallimard.

Index

Almond tart with pine
  nuts *30*
Artichoke hearts with young
  peas *28*
Artichoke mousse *74*
Artichoke terrine with a
  cream and chive sauce *14*
Asparagus cream soup with
  oysters *23*
Aubergine gratin *45*

Canard aux olives *26*
Celeriac purée *100*
Charlotte d'agneau au coulis
  de poivrons rouge *68*
Chicken sautéed young
  garlic *72*
Chocolate gâteau
  'l'Ardéchois' *111*
Chou vert à l'estragon *85*
Courgette gratin *55*

Dorade royale à la crème de
  romarin *97*

Fèves nouvelles à la menthe
  fraîche *19*
Filet de boeuf
  'Baumanière' *108*
Fillet of beef
  'Baumanière' *108*
Fillets of sea bream with a
  rosemary sauce *97*
Fillets of sole with a saffron
  sauce *80*

Fondant chaud au
  chocolat *20*
Fresh tuna à la
  Provençale *24*

Gâteau au chocolat
  'l'Ardéchois' *111*
Gigot d'agneau en croûte *18*
Gratin d'aubergines *45*
Gratin de courgettes *55*
Green bean salad with pan-
  fried sweetbreads *40*
Green cabbage with
  tarragon *85*

Hot chocolate creams *20*
Hot mint soufflé with
  chocolate sauce *57*

Lamb terrine with a red
  pepper sauce *68*
Leg of lamb in puff
  pastry *18*
Loup en croûte de sel, sauce
  estragon *70*

Mousseline d'artichauts *74*
Mussel soup *105*

Noisettes d'agneau aux
  olives *82*
Noisettes of lamb with
  olives *82*
Nougat glacé et son coulis
  de framboises *75*

Nougat parfait with a
    raspberry sauce *75*

Oeufs brouillés au caviar
    d'oursins *79*
Orange tart *86*

Petite nage de soles au
    safran *80*
Petite salade de truffes
    gourmande *96*
Petits farcis *49*
Pigeons au miel *44*
Pigeons roasted with
    honey *44*
Poached red mullet with a
    basil sauce *42*
Potato purée with olive
    oil *110*
Poulet sauté à l'ail
    nouveau *72*
Purée à l'huile d'olive de
    pomme de terre *110*
Purée de céléri rave *100*

Queue de lotte rôtie au
    four *107*

Râble de lapin rôti au
    basilic *54*
Ragoût de fonds d'artichauts
    aux petit pois *28*
Roast duck with olives *26*
Roast monkfish tail *107*
Roast saddle of rabbit with
    basil *54*
Rôti de thon frais à la
    Provençale *24*

Rouget poché à la nage au
    basilic *42*

Salade de haricots verts aux
    grillons de ris de veau *40*
Salmi of wild duck *98*
Salmis de canards
    sauvages *98*
Salmon with olives *16*
Saumon aux olives *16*
Scrambled eggs with sea
    urchins and caviar *79*
Seabass in a sea-salt crust
    with tarragon sauce *70*
Sorbet aux fraises *47*
Soufflé chaud à la menthe et
    sa sauce au chocolat *57*
Soupe de moules *105*
Spiced pear tarts *101*
Strawberry sorbet *47*
Stuffed Provençale
    vegetables *49*

Tarte aux pignons *30*
Tarte à l'orange
    'Baumanière' *86*
Tartes aux poires et aux
    epices caramelisées *101*
Terrine d'artichauts à la
    crème de ciboulette *14*
Truffle salad *96*
Turbot en bourride *52*
Turbot with aïoli *52*

Velouté d'asperges aux
    huitres *23*

Young broad beans with
    mint *19*

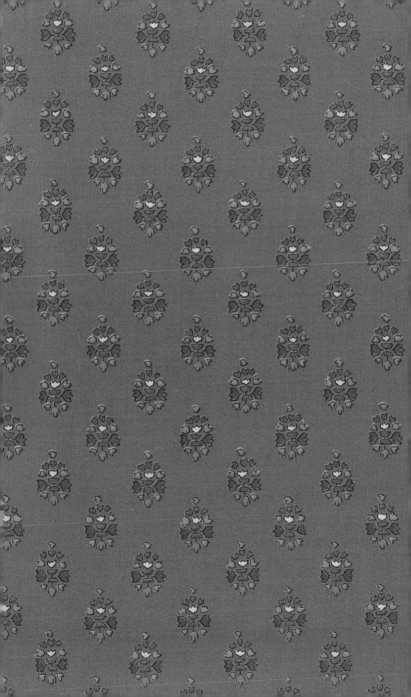